OTTAWA REFLECTIONS OF THE PAST

NELSON, FOSTER and SCOTT LTD., TORONTO, CANADA

DECEMBER/74

Dear Andrée and Walter

MERRY CHRISTMAS!

Love,
Simonne.

ISBN-0-919324-20-7

PREFACE

Was it Solomon who wrote "Of the making of books there is no end"? In recent years this could appear to be true of Ottawa. Flyleafs, pamphlets, posters, booklets, full-bodied books have come off the presses in volume — folklore, exploration, anecdotal, travel, technical, political, scientific, biographical, utterly fictional — name it and we seem to have it, each offering such a different Ottawa, you just can't believe your eyes!

But Eric Minton submits a different challenge — knowing and loving his Ottawa, he avers "Seeing is Believing". From the official archival photos of our Country, he offers you Ottawa as she was, and is, and hopes to be. He writes from knowledge and deep affection of his own very lovely old town, crowned with the towers of time and a not ignoble record of achievement, in which I have been privileged to share briefly as a controller, 1951, an alderman, 1969-1972 and for a decade in all as mayor, 1951-1956 and 1961-1964.

> CHARLOTTE WHITTON
> C.B.E., O.C., M.A., D.C.L., LL.D

In compiling this volume of photos of Ottawa, old and new, many people have been helpful: Mr. Richard Huyda and his staff in the Picture Division, Historical Photographs Section, Public Archives of Canada, Dr. Mary Burns, National Capital Commission, and the staff photographers, Mr. Bill Cadzow and Miss Betty Taylor at Central Mortgage and Housing Corporation. My thanks, also, to *The Ottawa Journal* and to Central Mortgage and Housing Corporation for permission to use material from their files. Special thanks are due to friends who said, "Why don't you put it all together in a book." Mr. George Foster kindly agreed. Here then are the results.

ERIC MINTON

Especially for the "Silver Maples" Library

Eric Minton

Nov/74

THE HILL

QUEEN VICTORIA'S BIRTHDAY, MONDAY, MAY 24, 1868

5

DUFFERIN BRIDGE, 1872

This vital link, connecting Rideau and Wellington Streets across the Rideau Canal in the heart of the city, was opened on October 23, 1873, by the Governor General, the Earl of Dufferin. City Council debated what to call the new structure until the last possible moment. As a result, the Earl was able to pause only briefly on his way to opening the session of Parliament saying, "I confess that the honour you have done me in calling upon me to name the bridge is unexpected and I would ask leave to defer taking advantage of that privilege until I can give it more consideration". *The Ottawa Times* then suggested that the

Governor General honour the bridge with his own name and so the new structure came to be known as Dufferin Bridge.

CONFEDERATION SQUARE
LOOKING SOUTH, 1974

In 1912, the first canal crossing, Sappers' Bridge (which had been built by Colonel John By's men in 1827) and Dufferin Bridge, were replaced, and the area was renamed Connaught Place after the resident Governor-General. The press of the day, however, ignored the name and called it Confederation Square. The public opted simply for The Plaza. Union Station, originally the Grand Trunk Railway Station, or simply Central Station, opened on Saturday, June 1, 1912, with no less than eight trains a day on the Grand Trunk line between Ottawa and Montreal. The CPR operated a further six. It truly was the age of railway travel. Today, the former railway station, handsomely refurbished, serves as the government Conference Centre. In the background is the new National Defence Headquarters building.

WELLINGTON STREET LOOKING
WEST, c. 1874

In the centre of this old photograph,
St. Andrew's Presbyterian Church is
seen under construction. Services
were held in the first church on the
site in September, 1828. The present
building was erected in 1873. Note,
in this view, the steeple has yet to be
added.

In the foreground, the buildings on
Parliament Hill are still under
construction. Work has been
underway since Tuesday, December
20, 1859; but, the final landscaping
will not be completed until 19 years
later — 1878. This accounts for the
incomplete look as the work slowly
progresses.

WELLINGTON STREET LOOKING
WEST, c. 1974

The spire of St. Andrew's is still visible although now surrounded on all sides by relatively new growth. The Confederation Building, right, was begun in 1927, Canada's Diamond Jubilee of Confederation Year, and the cornerstone was laid by Governor-General Viscount Willingdon. In 1973, it was renovated, at considerable cost, to accommodate Members of Parliament and their staff. There were many questions in the House over the expenditures.

Looming in the background is the new Holiday Inn and Place de Ville, the latter a commercial development by the Campeau Corporation that, with a network of hotels, cinemas, office towers, and an underground shopping mall, has transformed centre town west of Bank Street. In the foreground, the gates leading to the West Block on The Hill are one of the few legacies of the past in this area of old Ottawa.

THE CITY SKYLINE, c. 1866

This view, possibly taken from the old Court House on Nicholas Street, clearly indicates that the new buildings on The Hill constituted Ottawa's only skyline at that time. The West Block, barely recognizable here, was greatly enlarged in 1878; but, the East Block remains relatively unchanged to this day. The Library of Parliament, on which construction has just begun, did not open until 1876. The opening festivities included a grand ball given by the Quebec Members of the House of Commons. *The Daily Citizen* gave a lengthy account of the event on Tuesday, February 29, noting that "over 1,500 people attended and it was only with the greatest difficulty that dancing was kept up. Although refreshments were served at midnight, the dancing programme was not completed until four o'clock this morning at which time the ball broke up, everyone agreeing that the event passed off most enjoyably".

THE CITY SKYLINE FROM NICHOLAS STREET, 1971

"LONG MAY SHE REIGN OVER US", JUNE 22, 1897

The Ottawa Citizen continued below that opening headline on the great occasion of Queen Victoria's Diamond Jubilee, "Ottawa never looked gayer and brighter. Sparks and Rideau are long avenues of floating festoons and waving flags by day and at night a blaze of light. In the morning all the bells in the city began to peal at 8:00 a.m., although the press indicated that right thinking people had been up by six at the latest. There was a school concert on Parliament Hill, a review of the troops by the Governor-General on Cartier Square later, and in the afternoon a lacrosse game between the Capitals and the Shamrocks. The Capitals won. In the evening, a dance in the Drill Hall was vetoed at the last moment, but there were fireworks and an open air concert on The Hill." And there were the illuminations! *The Ottawa Citizen* put it this way, "The electrical exhibits on the principal streets were grand and that on Parliament Hill, marvellously beautiful." The Governor-General, that day, announced one work that would form a memorial of the Jubilee for the whole of Canada, the establishment of the Victorian Order of Nurses. The press deemed this "most fitting indeed".

THE CENTRE BLOCK, SEPTEMBER,
c. 1901

In 1901, Ottawa had a population of
60, 689. Contemporary accounts
estimate that half the city, some
30,000 people, turned out that
September when the Royal visitors
were in the city to see the new
illuminations which were part of the
great occasion. The press called it
"the work of a magician", and so it
must have seemed for at eight o'clock
The Hill was darkened and then
suddenly there it was — the whole
Centre Block outlined in electric
lights. And there was more! Major's
Hill Park, Sappers' Bridge and
Dufferin Bridge were covered with
lanterns. The Post Office was

illuminated and the famed Russell
Hotel had a huge sign in lights that
spelled out "Welcome".

THE DUKE AND DUCHESS OF YORK
WITH SIR WILFRID AND
LADY LAURIER,
SEPTEMBER, 1901

The Ottawa Journal called this
long-ago Royal visit "a howling
success" and added "we hope the
Duke and Duchess feel the same
way". The Royal visitors had come to
express their appreciation for
Canada's participation in the South
African War and also to unveil the
new statue on The Hill
commemorating the long reign of
Queen Victoria. Although the
ceremony was brief, security was
tight and *The Journal* noted "The Hill
fairly bristled with detectives and
secret service men from Montreal,
Toronto, and Ottawa."

The ceremony itself was simple. The
veil fell away, and the Duke made a
brief speech lasting just over one
minute and audible only in the
immediate vicinity. Nevertheless, it
was a moving occasion and the
crowd spontaneously broke into the
National Anthem. As a reporter noted,
"they sang it with a will, everyone
present from cabinet minister to
boot-black."

THE "SUNSHINE" PRINCE, SEPTEMBER 1, 1919

That's what *The Ottawa Journal* called the Duke of Windsor when he first came to Ottawa as the Prince of Wales in 1919. The excitement began on August 28 at 11:00 a.m. when the young man arrived at the Union Station to be greeted by what the paper called "the wildest enthusiasm and happiness that has ever been witnessed in the capital."

After what was officially described as a "quiet weekend", the main event of the Ottawa visit came on Monday, Labour Day, when the cornerstone was laid, by the Prince of Wales, for the new Victory Tower, the original name in the press for the Peace Tower. More than 35,000 people went wild as the Prince mixed and mingled with the veterans who had come back from the Great War.

Later, the Prince informally visited New York City, a welcome change after all the elaborate ceremony of the Canadian visit. The glitter of the Ziegfeld Follies was just one delight that the Prince took in while visiting the metropolis. He enjoyed the show so much that one number had to be repeated. Such encores were unknown, but this was an exception that the American showman was glad to make for his British visitor.

THE CENTRE BLOCK OF THE
PARLIAMENT BUILDINGS IN
FLAMES THURSDAY NIGHT,
FEBRUARY 3, 1916

"Did Hun Conspirators Start the
Fire?" That was the headline in *The
Ottawa Journal* on February 4, and
rumours were rampant.

The Fire Chief told *The Journal* that in
his opinion, "the fire was set and well
set. I distinctly heard five explosions
the like of which I never heard before
at a fire. I'm sure they were shells." In
another news story, the Liberal
member, Mr. E.M. MacDonald, stated
that during the dinner recess, about
an hour before the fire, his attention
was drawn to "a suspicious looking
foreigner, looking very intently down
the East Corridor. Suddenly the man
disappeared. Half-an-hour later the
building was in flames." That story
was topped by the reader who
reported that he met five men on Bank
Street, speaking German and each
carrying a small black bag. These
men, the reader was sure, were
responsible for the fire. Behind the
scenes, a hastily appointed Royal
Commission investigated the events
of the night of the fire. A report was
tabled on May 15, 1916, and although
it was inconclusive, there were strong
hints of incendiarism. To this day
stories about what really happened
still circulate.

COLONEL CHARLES LINDBERGH IN OTTAWA, JULY 2, 1927

The great Canadian event back in the summer of 1927 was the Diamond Jubilee of Confederation. On The Hill the new Carillon rang out for the first time while down at the street level a series of horse-drawn floats made their way through downtown Ottawa.

But these events, stirring though they were, took second place to the in-person appearance of the hero of the hour, "Lucky Lindy".

His solo flight on May 20 across the Atlantic had caught the attention of the whole world, and here he was in Ottawa, little more than a month later! *The Ottawa Journal* was there and their reporter wrote, "Wearing a double-breasted blue serge suit,

Lindbergh looked almost like a tall school boy", and on the following Monday an editorial noted, "It was hard to say whether Colonel Lindbergh's appearance was a disappointment to the great crowd. Heard on every side was the exclamation 'Why he's only a boy!' That was the predominant impression. He certainly did not look his 25 years."

But for the ladies in this photo, critical comment was superfluous. This was obviously a big moment for them.

PRIME MINISTER MACKENZIE KING
AND GUESTS, FEBRUARY 11, 1943

During the Second World War, the
government lost no opportunity to
boost morale with entertainment for
the armed forces and the general
public. Here the Prime Minister, a
keen devotee of stage and screen
when time permitted, is at his jovial
best as he greets Jack Benny and
Mary Livingstone. They appeared
with Jack's radio gang, Don Wilson,
Dennis Day and Rochester, at the old
Auditorium on O'Connor Street,
between special performances
performed for men and women in
uniform.

At an earlier date, Mr. King had the
pleasure of entertaining the
celebrated acting team of Alfred Lunt
and Lynn Fontanne when they
appeared in Ottawa in their great
stage success "There Shall Be No
Night". The Prime Minister held a
reception for the stars at Laurier
House after the performance. From all
accounts Mr. King greatly enjoyed
these occasional forays into the world
of show business.

A DIFFERENCE OF OPINION
ON THE HILL,
AUGUST 30, 1973

CONFEDERATION SQUARE SOMETIME DURING WORLD WAR 1

CONFEDERATION SQUARE

SPARKS STREET AT ELGIN, c. 1875

Sparks Street was planned along its present lines back in 1849, complete with a wooden sidewalk, on the south side only. At the same time one of the town's original cemeteries was transferred to the wilds of Rideau Street east, and a new business district was begun in what was then called Upper Town.

In the mid-1870s, Elgin Street on the west side, first block, housed *The Free Press*, near Wellington Street, and James Hope & Co., books and stationery, at the Sparks Street corner. Both institutions, albeit somewhat disguised, are still in business.

The Free Press merged with *The*

Ottawa Journal in 1917 and Hope's location at 61 Sparks Street is now occupied by W.H. Smith & Sons. Today, this historic block on Elgin Street contains the Langevin Building (1883), the first government building constructed off The Hill, and the Central Post Office (1938).

CONFEDERATION SQUARE LOOKING WEST, 1877

The handsome Post Office in the background is one year old. In the foreground, the Ottawa City Passenger Railway is plodding along, all of seven years old. The new transit service got under way with four horse-drawn cars at five o'clock on the morning of July 21, 1870, with a trial run over the new line that ran from New Edinburgh to the Chaudiére Falls. While labourers made a number of last minute repairs, the cars made their first trip for the public about five o'clock that same afternoon. Editorially, the new Street Railway came in second to Lisa Weber, "The Queen of Burlesque", who was appearing that same evening at the Music Hall. Press comment in *The Times* was brief, but to the point, "The Street Railway is now an established fact. After the delays and disappointments that have occurred and the many obstacles that have had to be overcome, the Company has nevertheless allowed nothing to halt the enterprise." Everything seemed quite satisfactory to the citizens and the new cars were for a time the subject of street-corner conversation.

CONFEDERATION SQUARE
LOOKING EAST, 1896

Great changes are about to take place on this side of Confederation Square. On the left, Dominion Park runs right up to Dufferin Bridge. On the right, three field pieces unofficially guard both the Rideau Canal and Wm. Howe, the paint manufacturer. By 1909, the railway tracks of the Canada Atlantic Railway run along side the canal to the new small centre town depot.

In that same year a new company, The Ottawa Terminals Railway Company, was formed in an attempt to bring some order out of the general railway confusion. The proposed solution was a large new central station on a site that had been eyed by railway magnates as early as the 1850s. These grand plans ultimately saw the demolition in 1912 of both Dufferin and Sappers' Bridges. Sappers' Bridge had been built to last. It was demolished in July 1912. Said *The Free Press* on July 23rd, "So hard was the stone and cement that even dynamite failed to wreck it". The contractors then used a derrick to hoist up a block of stone weighing about two tons to a height of fifty feet and then let it drop. After three hours of this tactic the whole bridge finally collapsed into the canal with a roar that could be heard all over the city.

SPARKS STREET AT ELGIN, c. 1898

The electric street car, new in Ottawa since June 29, 1891, had the right-of-way on Sparks Street at the turn of the century. In this view, the street has been macadamized from Bank Street to the Post Office. The start of the macadamizing project took place on July 30, 1895, with Mayor Borthwick officiating, complete with a silver shovel for the great occasion. The completion of the work by August 26th that same year was celebrated by a bicycle race which took place as the press reported under the new electric arc lights. *The Ottawa Journal* commented with a cogent editorial which read in part, "After the asphalt, the next problem is to keep it clean. This fact alone will prove decisive in the development of motor vehicles, once these get a start. To have the streets occupied only by silent rubber-tired vehicles with little mud and no manure will be an extremely pleasant improvement in city life. And this era is coming".

THE OTTAWA FIRE DEPARTMENT'S "CONQUERER", 1874

Fire was an ever present menace in old Ottawa. In 1869, on a cold winter night, the Court House went up in flames. *The Ottawa Times* reported, "The Fire engines turned out, but were frozen on the spot". On August 19th, 1870, the great Carleton County fire swept right up to Dow's Lake, forcing the city council to call out every able-bodied man.

The following year, the infamous Chicago holocaust did nothing to calm local fears.

On July 29, 1872, *The Free Press* carried a two-column story headed "TERRIBLE DISASTER". It read "A business block on Sussex Street went up in flames and worse still, there was a disgraceful row between the two rival volunteer fire brigades, the 'Centrals' and the 'Sapeurs'. While they fought each other, the public helped themselves freely to the stock of liquors at Dufresne's and McGarity's and then boasted of what they had done towards saving property and treated themselves for the aid they had rendered till they had dropped in the streets." Change came in 1874. In December, the Fire Department was organized on a municipal basis. There were five stations, each now connected with a new automatic alarm system, and to help out, by the end of the year the new fire hydrants were in place. Under Ottawa's first Fire Chief, William Young, eighteen professional fire fighters stood ready for any emergency.

THE RUSSELL HOTEL, c. 1898

At the close of the 19th and in the early years of the 20th century, the Russell Hotel at the south-east corner of Sparks and Elgin Streets, was the most famous hostelry in the city. Oscar Wilde was in town in 1882 and that celebrated beauty, Lillian Russell, signed the register in January, 1908. The hotel began as the Campbell House in 1845, a three storey structure with a tin roof and an attic that also contained rooms. Changes to the building and its name came with the selection of Ottawa as the Capital of the new Dominion.

The Russells were Americans who had been in the hostelry business in Quebec City when it was the temporary capital of the nation. They followed the seat of government to the new location in Ottawa and with James Gouin as Manager, opened for business in 1863. Thomas D'Arcy McGee was an early guest.

As the new civil service moved into the city, business boomed. The hotel was convenient to The Hill and the "Hotel Bar" became famous in an age of patronage and favour. To take care of the politicians and the lobbyists, the premises had to be enlarged not once, but three times in the 1870s and 1880s. We see it here at the height of its glory in the 1890s.

THE RUSSELL HOTEL FIRE
SUNDAY, APRIL 15, 1928

Saturday, April 14, 1928, was a memorable evening in Ottawa. A spectacular all-night fire destroyed the famous Russell Hotel. The building had recently been acquired by the Federal District Commission, now the National Capital Commission, and was destined to be razed at an early date to make way for a newly proposed Confederation Park. The main portion of the hotel was completely destroyed, but the Russell Theatre on the Queen Street side was undamaged. At the time of the fire the hotel had actually been vacant for some years having closed its doors on October 1, 1925 on surprisingly short notice and with little fanfare. The last of the guests checked out at 1:30 P.M. and the front door was padlocked.

The Russell Theatre, which had been expropriated, also closed in April, 1928. "The Dumbells", a favourite Canadian war-time revue, was the last stage show before the curtain was lowered permanently.

CIRCUS PARADE, CONFEDERATION SQUARE, c. 1906

THE CHATEAU LAURIER HOTEL AND THE UNION STATION
UNDER CONSTRUCTION, 1911

THE CHATEAU LAURIER NEARING COMPLETION, 1911

THE CHATEAU LAURIER, 1912

One summer day in 1912, the editor of *The Ottawa Journal* was challenged to a duel, aviator Wilbur Wright died, aerial mail service was tried out between New York and Washington, men's summer suits were on sale for $15.00 and 600 Ottawa carpenters and labourers went out on strike. The strikers wanted the princely wage of thirty-five cents an hour and a 9-hour day; but, labourers were willing to settle for thirty cents.

These news items are from the front page of *The Ottawa Journal* of Monday, June 3rd. Buried deep inside the paper on page 12 was a short one-column news item headed "Chateau Now Open". With that brief bow, the world-famous hotel opened for business.

The first name signed in the hotel register on that June afternoon was that of Sir Wilfrid Laurier. But as *The Journal* noted at the time, aside from his presence, there was a complete absence of ceremony. In the stiff journalese of the period, the news item went on: "No sooner were the doors open on Saturday afternoon then began a stream of visitors that continued late into the evening. More than 500 people visited the new hotel. In the evening the spacious dining room was well-filled. Exclamations of wonder and surprise were heard on all sides. That it is rivalled by few and surpassed by none was an opinion expressed by many".

"FINEST ARTILLERY BRIGADE IN CANADA GOES TO THE FRONT"

That was the headline in *The Ottawa Journal* that day in late August, 1914, when the first troops began to leave the city. The story went on: "From the Exhibition Grounds to the Union Station friends turned out to see the 'Princess Pats' as they passed. The name 'Princess Pat's' or more correctly 'Princess Patricia's Canadian Light Infantry' was conferred on the regiment by the Governor General, the Duke of Connaught's daughter, who lent her assistance in raising a regiment at the outbreak of the First World War.

From windows flags waved and a crowd of Ottawa Collegiate Institute boys gave their comrades a hearty yell. The send-off was affecting. Men rushed out to shake hands with the boys on the guns and everyone present proceeded to Confederation Square where police reinforcements were required to keep the people back. In all 295 horses, 8 guns, and 6 wagons were loaded onto the trains."

THE 'PRINCESS PAT'S' RETURN HOME, MARCH, 1919

KING GEORGE VI AND QUEEN ELIZABETH UNVEILING THE NATIONAL WAR MEMORIAL — SUNDAY, MAY 21, 1939

After the Diamond Jubilee of Confederation in 1927, Royal Visits lapsed for a decade or more. Headlines and breadlines took over in the 1930s; but, in May, 1939, on the eve of World War II, there was a cross-Canada Royal Tour that is a legend to this day.

In Ottawa, the events began with a full page photo of the royal couple on the front page of *The Ottawa Journal* on Saturday, May 3rd.

Under the photo the editor wrote, "If Ottawa had a Rip Van Winkle who had slept for two months who wakened on the steps of the National War Memorial he would be amazed. Back in March, Connaught Place was 'Hell's Half Acre'. Today the widening of Elgin Street and the completion of the Memorial is a triumph of organization; downtown has been transformed. It is as surprising as it is beautiful."

Sunday, May 21st, was the final day in Ottawa and the most moving as the whole city jammed downtown to see Their Majesties officially unveil the new Memorial. Here protocol was tossed aside as the couple moved among the veterans. There was a 40-minute get-together with the "old sweats" who had fought in the 1914-1918 conflict. "Shake", said one swarthy old-timer, as he grinned his welcome to the Queen. She shook. That weekend is still remembered as one of the great moments in the on-going Ottawa story.

"V.J." NIGHT AT THE NATIONAL WAR MEMORIAL, AUGUST, 1945.

MAYOR STANLEY LEWIS AND BARBARA ANN SCOTT,
CONFEDERATION SQUARE, MARCH 9, 1948

"Back Home in Triumph" headlined *The Ottawa Citizen* and a full-page story followed. "In the biggest spontaneous demonstration this city has ever seen, Ottawa's own Barbara Ann Scott returned like a queen. No Roman conqueror returning from his greatest hour ever got more vociferous acclaim than did the Olympic, European, and World skating champion. But here were no victims chained to chariot wheels.

Here instead were loyal Ottawans tied to Barbara Ann's heart strings. Today may not have been a holiday in the statutory sense — but Ottawa people took a holiday just the same. It was a holiday of the heart and not of the calendar." Barbara Ann had been an Ottawa favourite since the days when she had skated in the local Minto Follies, and a growing public had followed her career every step of the way to her triumph in February,

1948, at the Winter Olympics in Switzerland.

After this crowning achievement, Miss Scott skated for several seasons with the Hollywood Ice Revue before retiring. As she put it, candidly, "I want to learn to cook." She also married and today lives in Chicago. In her hometown, she will always be remembered.

CONFEDERATION SQUARE, 1972

49

CENTRE TOWN SKYLINE LOOKING NORTH, 1971

UPPER TOWN

TOWN MEETING, AUGUST, 1868

In Bytown, as Ottawa was first known, the regular Municipal Council met in the Town Clerk's office over a store on Rideau Street. On August 21, 1849, a motion was carried that the upper part of the West Ward Market Building, on Elgin Street, be fitted out as a town hall. In 1848, this wooden building, with outside stairs on both sides, had been built for a market. When the building became the Town Hall, a fire brigade was placed on the ground floor together with a police station.

For many years, the old council chamber on the second floor served as a meeting place, political arena, and theatre where lectures, concerts and temperance meeting were held. The old Town Hall remained in use until 1878.

In the photograph, a meeting to discuss the necessity of installing a city-owned waterworks system is convening. The 'water carriers' who would be put out of business by the new system, were out in force. They pointed out that in view of the City's poor financial situation, the time was not suitable for such an expensive project. The meeting ended in fist fights and general disorder. The "nays" won!

THE PARLIAMENTARY LIBRARY,
1916

This is a most unusual view of the
Parliamentary Library and probably
the only one in existence that shows
the building from Wellington Street
without the intrusion of the Centre
Block. The cameraman obviously
took advantage of the destruction by
fire of the Centre Block in February,
1916, and the subsequent demolition
of the shell of the old building to
catch on film this unique view. The
Rideau Club, left, and the Langevin
Block, right, are still in place, but
those cars were long ago snapped up
by antique car enthusiasts.

SPARKS STREET CORNER OF BANK, c. 1910

THE SPARKS STREET MALL, MID-SUMMER, 1971

R.J. DEVLIN'S QUEEN STREET
ENTRANCE, 1910

Bob Devlin opened a hat shop on March 9, 1869 at No. 1 Sappers' Bridge and the firm remained in business from that date until 1951. Bob Devlin had a winning Irish way and a quick wit, and with the new Civil Service filling the small city and Parliamentarians arriving from the most remote constituencies, business could only improve. And it did. In 1891, he built this handsome store at number 74 Sparks which ran through to Queen Street. The Devlin advertisements in the Ottawa press in the 1890 s became famous. In the days before cartoons and comics, many readers turned first to the Devlin ad to see what Bob Devlin had to say about federal politics, municipal government, or such mundane matters as the state of Ottawa's streets! He wrote in one ad: "My business is located behind a rut on the south side of the street — not the small rut over by Elgin — but the large one near the middle of the block."

The Devlin advertisements poked and prodded City Council into actions that finally resulted in the adoption of improvements such as street lighting, paved roads and cement sidewalks, all of which were lacking when the new store first opened on Sparks Street.

THE WINDSOR HOTEL, METCALFE
STREET AT QUEEN, 1909

The haven of the commercial
traveller opened in 1872 as the St.
James Hotel. A year later it acquired
a new name, the Daniels' Hotel. The
new owner, Samuel Daniels,
renamed the building the Windsor
House in the mid-1870s and that
name stuck, remaining with the hotel
until the old property was acquired
and demolished by the Royal Bank of
Canada as part of their new Sparks
Street offices in 1959.

The Windsor Hotel's great days are
long gone, but, history was made in
1892 when Thomas Ahearn, fresh
from introducing the electric street
car to Ottawa, pioneered the electric
stove. On Monday, August 29th, his
guests sat down to the first meal
cooked anywhere on an electric
stove. Ahearn's workshop served as
the kitchen, but the meal was served
in style in the Windsor dining room.

BOWLES LUNCH, 1917

Back in the 1920 s, when you could meet everyone you knew on Sparks Street, Bowles Lunch was a place where a man could grab a quick bite without fuss or ceremony. Although the clients had class the decor was strictly utilitarian. No fancy drapes, no soft music, no pretty waitresses in alarming décolletage, it was in fact a 'one arm joint'. This terminology arose from the fact that along both sides of the room, there were a series of chairs, each complete with a small enameltop table on one arm. On this small table you balanced coffee and whatever else you had ordered. Service was cafeteria-style, and before they installed a sound system, the waiter bawled the orders back into the kitchen in a jargon peculiar to such ''beaneries'' and more redolent of Damon Runyan than the Oxford Dictionary. Bowles never closed; they were open 24 hours a day. Nice girls did not go to this masculine haunt and after a late evening out, only a brash young man would ask his girl friend to have breakfast at Bowles.

REGENT THEATRE
JANUARY 9, 1972

This Disney revival was the last show at the old Regent Theatre, a squat blockhouse of a building that stood for 57 years on the north-west corner of Bank Street at Sparks. Though it may have been an architectural monstrosity it was, nevertheless, the city's leading motion picture theatre for years, showing the very best of both Hollywood and foreign films. It opened for business in January, 1916, and for years played week after week to packed houses, particularly after the introduction of sound films in December, 1928. The first film with sound (music only) was "The Street Angel", starring Janet Gaynor and Charles Farrell. In March, 1929, the first "all-talking, all-singing, all-dancing" screen musical arrived at the Regent. The "Broadway Melody" was the film and it had the crowds lining up to Wellington Street waiting to get in. Those were great days for this old theatre.

In 1972, the building was demolished.

THE MOTOR AGE ARRIVES AT THE CORNER OF BANK AND SPARKS STREETS, 1905

Harry Walker, the well-known Ottawa historian notes: "It is practically impossible to determine the order of precedence of the first cars in Ottawa. Certainly among the first owners were: W. Bronson, E.C. Grant, Thomas Ahearn, Fred Dunning, George Millen, Harry Brouse, and the Ketchum's."

The Ottawa Free Press on September 11, 1900, reported that the first auto had been seen on Sparks Street, an electric car, a Stanhope, with a lady driver at that! Mrs. Thomas Ahearn was at the wheel on the occasion and the car performed so well that the owners made a run out to Britannia, a nearby summer resort, that same day. The following year gasoline driven cars were on the streets and when the first trucks arrived in 1907, purchased by the E.B. Eddy Company, that news ran side by side with the fact that Sarah Bernhardt was in town!

BRYSON, GRAHAM AND COMPANY,
SPARKS STREET AT O'CONNOR,
1892

Bryson, Graham and Company, an old Ottawa institution began initially at 110 Sparks Street in 1878 with Charles Bryson as the proprietor. A new company with the more lengthy name to take in Bryson's partner, F.J. Graham, moved into this corner location about 1880.

Located in the heart of the city, business boomed and gradually the company took over adjoining premises until, by 1900, the store ran from 142 to 152 Sparks Street with a side entrance on O'Connor and also on Queen Streets.

Having grown piecemeal up Sparks Street over the years and on a slight incline, the store became, with time, a veritable labyrinth of aisles, archways and steps. It did not close its doors even in the face of change and new and modern merchandising methods until April 18, 1953.

SHARRY'S, SPARKS STREET AT O'CONNOR, 1973

Bryson, Graham's is gone, but a trace of the old company remains in this corner restaurant, which was originally established by the store in the mid-1930s as one of the final bids made by management to keep up with the times. The original buildings that made up Bryson, Graham's remain hidden behind new modern facades and are completely refurbished throughout. Only this corner dining room harks back to an earlier era.

SUN LIFE BUILDING, SPARKS STREET CORNER OF BANK, 1908

Today, you can barely recognize the old Sun Life Building on the south-east corner of Bank and Sparks Streets in downtown Ottawa; but, in 1898, when it was designed by architect E.L. Horwood, it was one of the main business blocks in centre town. Horwood, later Chief Architect for the Department of Public Works during the years 1914-1918, began his practice in 1895. This famous old structure on the corner of Bank and Sparks was one of his first major successes in the city. The style of the architecture, complete with cupola and a large bronze statue of Mercury, capture the period perfectly.

Horwood followed this with the Citizen Building on Sparks Street, the high wedge-shaped National Building at the top of Rideau Street next to the Union Station and the original Carnegie Library on Metcalfe Street. All subsequent structures have vanished with time, but the building on the corner of Bank and Sparks remains. In 1950-51, the building was largely remodelled and refurbished to its present-day look. The Victorian cupola vanished and the statue of Mercury disappeared into the Bytown Historical Museum, where it remains to this day — a very special attraction.

SPARKS STREET CORNER OF BANK, 1970

Horwood's Sun Life Building has been greatly altered inside and out, but it still stands on this busy corner and is in daily use. On the opposite side of the street is the Canadian Head Office of the Metropolitan Life Insurance Company built in 1924. The main entrance to this relatively new building is on Wellington Street and on the Sparks Street side, a row of smart shops brightens this end of the Mall.

In 1973, the Federal Government announced that this property had been expropriated as part of the long range planning for the core area of centre town, but with the reassurance that what ever form this planning may ultimately take, the merchants on Sparks Street will be left relatively undisturbed.

THE ROBERT SIMPSON COMPANY AND THE MALL THEATRE, 1973

The Robert Simpson business began here as Murphy-Gamble's department store on March 10, 1910. When it opened as "Ottawa's Colossal Store", according to front page stories in the newspapers of the day, the police had to be called out to handle the tremendous crowds. The premises were so big that the top floor was left vacant. It later became the location of the Rideau Room restaurant. The original owners were the John Murphy Company Limited, a Montreal-based firm, and Samuel Gamble, managing director of this early Ottawa department store.

The Mall Theatre opened in October, 1915, as the Centre Theatre and for years it was one of Ottawa's premier film houses. Time and television, however, took their toll and the doors closed in 1973.

Both the store and the theatre are scheduled for demolition and present plans call for a new and much more "colossal" store to be built on the site.

MORGAN'S ON THE MALL, 1973

Morgan's, as the present generation knew it, has left The Mall, but old Ottawans remember when the name 'Devlin', in bold letters, was on the side of the building. It was one of the most exclusive stores in town.

When Morgan's took over the Devlin firm in 1951, the building was repainted, modernized throughout and given a contemporary look at street level. Both Devlin's and Morgan's are gone now. Detailed plans have not as yet been announced for the new structure to be built on the site.

Just after this photo was taken in 1973, the Carleton Chambers on the south side of Sparks Street, in the first block was demolished.

MISS LIVINGSTON c. 1875

On May 10 and 11, 1875, at the Rink Music Hall down on Slater Street by the canal, the main attraction was a pioneer burlesque show featuring Madame Rentz's Female Ministrels. As an added attraction, there were the delights of Mlle DeLacour's French Can-Can Dancers.

That same night at the Grand Opera House, T.C. King was performing in "Hamlet". The *Daily Citizen* reviewed "Hamlet" at length, but had to note lamely at the end that there were a lot of empty seats. The press shied away from the burlesque performance with only a one-sentence comment, "A

very large audience witnessed the efforts of the female ministrels last night; they give a second entertainment tonight." The press attended the burlesque show the second evening; no doubt in the interests of professional journalism. They noted that "this troupe was not so well patronized . . . as on the previous evening, the character of the entertainment being better understood."

One wonders, however, if the audience at the old Grand Opera House was any larger for Mr. King and "Hamlet".

MAYOR CHARLOTTE WHITTON
OPENING THE SPARKS STREET
MALL, 1963

In 1960, the Sparks Street Development Association, which was made up of the merchants and businessmen in the area, convinced city officials to establish a pedestrian Mall, on an experimental basis, for the summer months. The Provincial Government approved and so successful was this initial experiment that The Mall was placed on a permanent year-round basis in 1966. Two years later, city council approved an extension of two blocks westerly to Lyon Street to take in the new Place de Ville development.
In 1974, construction is still under way on the site of the old Regent Theatre. When this is complete, there will be a pedestrian walkway across centre town from Elgin Street to Lyon Street. The completion of this walkway will signify the complete renewal of this old core area of the city.

THE CAPITOL THEATRE,
OPENED NOVEMBER, 1920,
CLOSED MAY, 1970

LOWER TOWN

BYWARD MARKET c. 1911

Ed. ROBERT.

SUSSEX STREET, 1870

Rideau Street at Sussex Street once looked like this before the large Daly Building at the corner was constructed in 1905. This building was used first as a department store and then as government offices. On the west side of Sussex Street, opposite George Street, stood the Anglican Chapel of Ease, built in 1860. Later it was renamed the Church of St. John the Evangelist and, in 1912, was destroyed by fire. The large building across the street, although greatly altered, is still standing and in use as government offices.

The original building on Sussex Street, the British Hotel, was built in 1827. In 1853, it was largely rebuilt and in 1865, with the flurry of excitement over the designation of Ottawa as the capital, a large new wing extending along George Street was added. It was immediately requisitioned as a barracks for the British troops who came out to Canada with the first Governor General. After 1871, the building reverted to public use as the Clarendon Hotel.

In 1880, the building served as the nation's first National Gallery in which an exhibition of art was displayed by the newly formed Canadian Academy of the Arts. From this Academy grew the present National Gallery. Government interest in the building lingered after the exhibition and it has housed a variety of departments and services since 1881. The Geological Survey of Canada occupied the building from 1881 until the last members moved out in 1940.

RIDEAU STREET AT SUSSEX, 1875

Rideau Street was originally owned by Ottawa pioneer Nicholas Sparks who had bought 200 acres of property in the heart of the new community in June, 1821. In 1823, to control land speculation, the Crown bought 400 acres in the Rideau Canal and Lower Town area. As Harry Walker, the well-known Ottawa Valley historian points out, "Colonel John By practically took 104 acres from Nicholas Sparks under powers of expropriation conferred by the Rideau Canal Act." Both men collaborated in the laying out of the first two main streets in the new town, Wellington and Rideau. It was agreed that to the government strip 33' wide would be added a strip of Sparks' property 66' wide. In this way both streets are broad wide avenues to this day. Mr. Walker adds, "This can now be rated as the first sensible town planning project in the capital."

RIDEAU STREET AT SUSSEX, c. 1900

In the 1890s, the tracks of the Ottawa Electric Railway Company spread out in all directions. As early as 1891, permission had been received to run new car lines into Rockcliffe, and along Albert Street to the Broad Street Station, the new CPR depot.

That decade also saw the tracks laid on Nicholas Street and Laurier Avenue on the city's east side. On the west side, the bridge at Somerset Street was built and street-railway service to that section of the city began in April, 1896. By then, Rockcliffe had become a popular summer resort with cottagers commuting to and from the city on the new car line. The Rockcliffe line was

so successful that a new line to Britannia Park opened with fanfare and fireworks on May 24, 1900. It was the golden age of the street-car complete with open cars in the summer! People even talked seriously of a car line to Bells Corners.

In this view the open street car, fresh from a run to Rockcliffe, trundles up Rideau Street to Confederation Square. All the buildings on the right side of the street disappeared long ago. They, or their successors, were torn down as part of the general beautification of the area for Canada's Centennial Year.

RIDEAU STREET AT SUSSEX, 1973

The Transportation Building, immediately on the right of the photo, served for years as an interim City Hall until the handsome new building on Green Island was completed in 1958. In this area of Rideau Street, as we see it today, there is one old building that dates from the last century. Today the "Treble Clef" at 68 Rideau, is given over to Mozart or acid rock, take your choice, but in the 1870s the building was R.W. Steven's "English Hotel". Later in the same decade it was I.B. Taylor's printing office. Today the music may be modern; but, the building shows its true age in its pitched roof and dormers.

In the distance (the sign is half hidden by the traffic light) is the long-established firm of Charles Ogilvy. They originally opened for business on the south side, near their present site, on November 16, 1887.

RIDEAU STREET AT DALHOUSIE, c. 1930

The squat square building in the centre of this view is the Monument Nationale Theatre which was built in 1904. A second floor auditorium offered both stage and screen entertainment. The theatre's turn-of-the-century charm was preserved well into the post-World War II era. The long block behind it housed the well-remembered Francais Theatre, home of Buck Jones, Ken Maynard and Gene Autry.

RIDEAU STREET AT DALHOUSIE, 1974

"EARNSCLIFFE", SUSSEX STREET, 1967

Constructed about 1857, "Earnscliffe" was the home of Canada's first Prime Minister, Sir John A. Macdonald, from 1883 until his death in 1891.

Since 1928, "Earnscliffe" has been the home of the British High Commissioner to Canada.

BASILIQUE NOTRE-DAME d'OTTAWA

Construction of this famous Ottawa church began in 1841 when a contract was given to Antoine Robillard. Under the direction of Monseigneur Guigues the work proceeded slowly and in 1846 the church, which was built of stone, was consecrated. In 1858, the twin spires each 180' high, were added. Four years later the church itself was enlarged with the building of a choir, but the interior remained largely unfinished. This final stage in the building of this great Basilica got under way in 1878.

The interior woodwork in the sanctuary was crafted by Philippe Parizeau who also worked on some of the carving in the Library of Parliament.

The Basilica was connected in other ways to the life of the city. In the south tower of the church was a clock which, in the 1870s, was linked by telegraph with the clock in the old Tower of the Centre Block on The Hill. The marvel of telegraphy allowed the bells to ring simultaneously with the firing of the noon-day gun.

RIDEAU STREET, LOOKING EAST, c. 1958

The Daly Building, at the corner of Rideau and Sussex Streets, is to come down according to news items which have turned up with great regularity, in some form or another, since the building opened as Lindsay's Department Store on June 14, 1905. The original notice of the government's intention to expropriate the structure appeared in the press on June 2, 1905. The building still stands in 1974!

Built on the side of a hill, the slope of the street resulted in the first floor being partially underground. As a result, it was necessary to install prism glass to catch the sunlight. The store itself was lit throughout with arc lamps: electricity was reserved for the one elevator. A.E. Rae & Company took over management of the building in 1909 and added two stories and a new wing on the north side in 1913.

Actual use of the building by the government took place in World War I when it became Canadian Naval Headquarters. Later, in 1919, the building was used to house the Militia Records Office, the Bureau of Statistics, the Department of Public Health and the Ottawa Office of the Income Tax Department.

The National Building, on the opposite side of Rideau Street, was designed by architect E.L. Horwood and built about 1903. It was demolished in the redesign of the area in the mid-1960s.

LOWER TOWN URBAN RENEWAL, 1973

AROUND TOWN

OTTAWA FOOTBALL CLUB,
NOVEMBER, 1890

QUEEN'S PARK, AYLMER, QUEBEC, 1900

Aylmer, Quebec was an important year-round community long before the city of Hull became prominent. In the early days, stage coaches, operated by Moses Holt, ran between the two communities, but business really boomed in 1879 when the Quebec, Montreal, Ottawa and Occident Railway reached Aylmer. It was well on its way to becoming an important suburb.

At the same time the Hull Electric Railway Company established a line to Aylmer and at the turn of the century, a large amusement center called Queen's Park was established on the shore of Lake Deschenes with lake trips on the "G.B. Greene". This attractive spot was popular right from the start. Many Ottawans will recall the Hull Electric cars crossing into Ottawa via the Alexandra Bridge with the depot in Confederation Square beside the Chateau Laurier Hotel.

In 1900, a trip by train or street-railway to Aylmer was a full day's outing. But time has passed and the amusement and picnic center, the "J.B. Greene", and the Hull Electric are no longer in existence.

"COOKERY" ON J.R. BOOTH'S RAFT, OTTAWA RIVER, c. 1880

BRITANNIA-ON-THE-BAY, ONE OF OTTAWA'S FAVOURITE SUMMER RESORTS, c. 1900

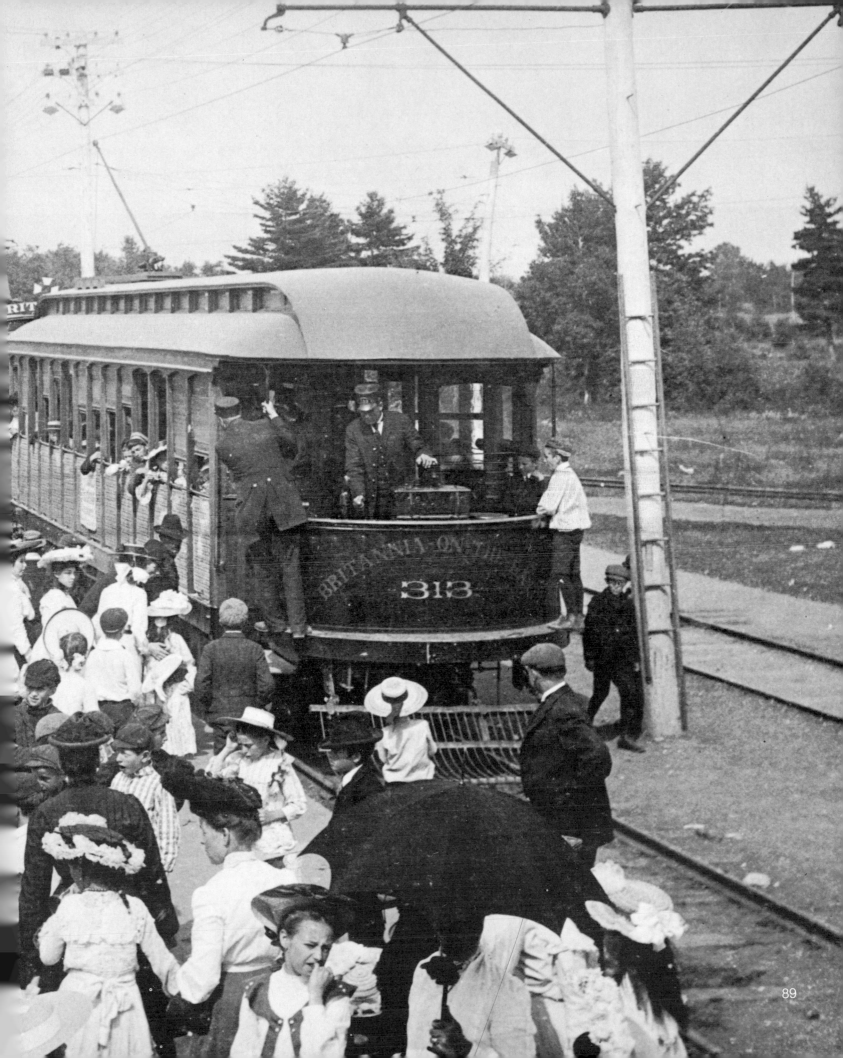

ELGIN STREET, LOOKING SOUTH
FROM WELLINGTON, c. 1900

In the last century, the east side of
Elgin Street was given over to
commerce. The Clisby House, at the
corner of Wellington, was followed
along the street by the Patent Office,
the Canadian Express Company, and
two clubs, The Carlton Club and The
Reform Association. Across Sparks
Street stood the impressive Russell
Hotel and beyond that, to the south,
the old City Hall. The Elgin Street
transformation as we know it today,
began in 1926 when the Federal
District Commission (now the
National Capital Commission) began
to clear the first block on the east side
of Elgin. This area was later known as
Plaza Park.

ELGIN STREET LOOKING SOUTH,
1973

The only building left over from an
earlier era on Elgin Street is the
commercial block which still stands
on the south-west corner of Sparks
Street. This structure, which dates
from the 1880s, is still relatively
unchanged nearly a century later.

THE OTTAWA RIVER AND THE
LUMBER MILLS FROM THE WEST
BLOCK, c. 1878

A century ago, some of the most
important people in Ottawa lived on
Cliff Street. Vittoria Street, seen here,
was equally fashionable. In this
enclave of the well-to-do lived some
of the Fathers of Confederation and,
at one time, the Anglican Bishop of
Ontario. His next door neighbour was
Prime Minister Alexander Mackenzie.

On this bluff overlooking the Ottawa
River the view must have been
unforgettable on at least two
occasions; once, in 1866, when an
aerial artist crossed the Chaudiére
Falls on a high-wire and later, in
1900, when the great fire of that year

roared out of Hull uncontrolled, and
consumed most of what was then the
west side of Ottawa, including the
lumber mills on both sides of the
river.

THE OTTAWA RIVER AND THE
SUPREME COURT BUILDING FROM
THE WEST BLOCK, 1970

Ottawa has been growing and
changing since Sir Wilfrid Laurier
conjured up his vision of the
"Washington of the North". The
Ottawa Improvement Commission
was appointed in 1899. In 1913, the
conservative administration of Sir
Robert Borden appointed a Federal
Plan Commission to look into the
whole question of an expanding
government as well as an expanding
city (the population in 1911 was
90,520). The Commission's report
was published in 1915 and it stated,
"The land west of the Parliament
Buildings to Bronson Avenue and the
land on the top of the cliff should be
used for departments of government.
Expansion along the Ottawa River
west of Parliament Hill is the logical
course, being out of the line of
commercial development. Here there
is offered splendid architectural
opportunity."

The Confederation Building on
Wellington Street at Bank and the
Justice Building, also on Wellington,
started a major transformation in the
area. This was greatly accelerated by
the building of the Supreme Court
Building in 1938. As construction
progressed the last vestiges of Cliff
and Vittoria Streets were eliminated.
The transformation of the area was
completed in May, 1939 when, during
the Royal Tour of Canada, Queen
Elizabeth laid the cornerstone for the
Supreme Court Building.

"CANAL SKATING DRAWS RECORD CROWD OF 94,000" — The Ottawa Journal, February 19, 1974

THE AUTHOR

Eric Minton, a resident of Ottawa since 1923, is a graduate of Queen's University, Kingston. He is presently employed by Central Mortgage and Housing Corporation in the nation's capital.

ACKNOWLEDGEMENTS

The Public Archives of Canada
National Capital Commission
Central Mortgage and
Housing Corporation
CP Picture Service
National Film Board of Canada

"Man with a Camera" Silhouette by Barry Johnston, Toronto.

Edited and designed by Mike Filey, author "Toronto, Reflections of the Past"
Printed by the Graphic Centre, Toronto
Bound by T.H. Best Ltd., Toronto